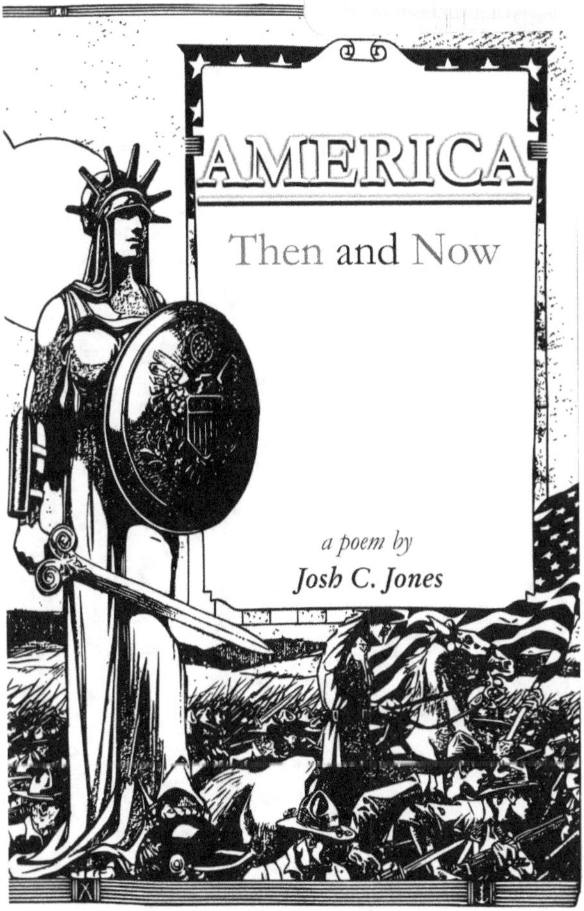

AMERICA

Then and Now

a poem by

Josh C. Jones

FMS BOOKS

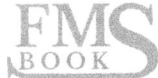

AMERICA

Then and Now

a poem by
Josh C. Jones

FMS Books

AMERICA

Then and Now

a poem by **Josh C. Jones**

ISBN: 979-8-9870614-2-8 (Paperback)
ISBN: 979-8-9870614-3-5 (Ebook)

All opinions expressed in this book by the author are, of course, the author's.

This book is generously gifted to

_____

By

_____

AMERICA
Then and Now

a poem by **Josh C. Jones**

CONTENTS

Dedication   xi

AMERICA: Then and Now (poem)   1

Pledge of Allegiance   23

Quotes   25

Special Note   38

DEDICATION

Thank you, LORD, for your divine wisdom and guidance instilled in our founders for the formation and foundation of the most prosperous, free, and "Life, Liberty, and the pursuit of Happiness" nation among men. As our Founding Fathers declared; "Providence," the "Creator," "Supreme Judge," and "Nature's God," who made all men equal and from whom we derive reason, morality, and liberty, granted us these unalienable, Natural, God-given rights. Rights which no man can in a just, moral, or right-minded way deprive us in America, so long as we remember our beginnings and continue to give thanks where thanks is due: to the only firm basis for liberty which is the belief that it was a gift of God, as Thomas Jefferson wrote in *Notes on the State of Virginia.*

July Fourth, 1776

"All societies of men must be governed in some way or the other. The less they may have a stringent state government, the more they must have of individual self-government. The less they rely on public law or physical force, the more they must rely on private moral restraint. Men, in a word, must necessarily be controlled either by a power within them, or by a power without them; either by the word of God, or by the strong arm of man; either by the Bible or the bayonet."

Robert C. Winthrop

I once believed what was said to me
From numerous heads floating free:
That to be what it is this country's to be
To not judge solely on race, religion, or belief;

That color be not a divider of free
Or a card to be played for diversity;
That upon merit of one's own person he
Be awarded advance, to that we agreed.

To treat all the same, to equal be—
Treat others as I wish them to treat me—
And this is where in truth we would see
How, as one nation under God, we live free.

This and much more were once preached
In this land of the brave and home of the free
By those who served officially
And reported the truth historically.

It was a land sought out to worship Thee
Free from oppression by feudality,
A place where man could decree
His own path and be serfdom-free.

Where learned folk could upswing
And common sense was guaranteed;
Self-evident was obvious, obviously;
And servants served the citizenry.

And it was taught educationally:
The Commandments of Ten and morality.
And even the media often unbiased be,
Though not without a few faults politically,

But more often than not, truthfully,
Facts and events were reported to thee;
Opinionated heads were not floating free—
Of course, then, there was no TV.

Biblical principles in public speech
By presidents, Congress, and family,
Schools, politics, and religion teach
That morality requires absolute foundationality;

That to know what is good and rightly
Requires a standard to compare thee;
Inspired Word they chose the light be
From where these standards grow uprightly.

Our founders were eruditely
Versed in politics and religiosity,
And having fought victoriously,
Birthed a nation experientially.

Oppression and isms, they rejected widely
And warned of corruption inwardly,
Which would despotism bring most likely
If the people became wicked, immorally.

And if absolute by popular opinion be
Found as intolerant and bigotry
By opinion of the people, not Constitutionally,
Then usurpation will destroy the free.

Our Constitution is inadequate, functionally,
If people, virtuous, no longer be;
Corruption, to wit, final arbiter, federal judiciary
Warnings if we lose foundational integrity.

Religion and morality indispensable be
For patriotism and political prosperity.
The stone rejected our cornerstone be
For Unalienable and Constitutionality.

It was self-evident that the principle of equality
Meant without consent no one may rule thee;
That God, our Creator, gave rights divinely
For a new nation formed through religiosity.

That a standard of good and morality
Must come from an absolute finality,
And a deviation from this foundationality
Would deprive truth of its reality,

Because from God these rights were divinely
Given so that man could not deprive thee,
And a beacon of light would shine brightly
For the oppressed to find shelter legally.

Because we knew nations without borders be
No nation that could claim sovereignty,
And without laws to distinguish from history,
Then tyranny would creep in freely.

We understood that there is an enemy
Who would seek to destroy our liberty,
And with no distinction between citizenry,
Then no rights could a Constitution guard thee.

We The People of the United States, be
The guardians for our posterity,
Not the elected to rule dictatorially,
A free people, not a kingly dynasty.

These truths were known, and we profoundly
Fought and sacrificed to change the world we
Lived so there would be a light shining brightly,
A beacon (hope) in a world shrouded so darkly.

Ever-striving land of representative democracy;
A Republic set forth for human decency;
Documents set forth for each person's liberty;
Education, each generation to learn from thee.

Freedom to worship and freedom to think;
Freedom to Life and freedom to speak;
Freedom to work and freedom to peace;
Freedom to defend life and family;

Freedom to earn and decline medically;

Freedom to give in earnest charity;

Freedom from coercion and from barbarity—

Freedom that was then only a rarity.

This was America, the land of the free,

A land and unique culture never before seen;

A nation of its own that would change history

And abolish a trade that all people sold thee.

Our foundation upon biblical proficiency.

Document, no mention of race, color, slavery.

Knowing and fighting for all men to be free

In a world so chained, extremists they be.

From a king, they fought to end such tyranny:

Deprive, incite, enslave, dividing citizenry;

Representation denied; a despot pro-slavery.

Freedom, they knew, worth more than security.

They knew that to seek security over liberty
Meant continued oppression, perceived safety,
And to seek safety over liberty be
To have neither in objective reality.

They sacrificed all so we could be free
To think and speak and live in liberty.
The wisdom they showed, the credit decreed,
A foundation they laid, penned conventionally.

Conspiracy theorists, in their warnings, we read
Of infiltration through groups politically
To subvert the nation's morality
And affirm a foundation of ambiguity.

Freedom they knew was worth preserving;
Truth was upon which they were building;
And each, by action, they showed courageously,
Was paramount to Life and Liberty.

8

Through founding documents, it was decreed:
Our rights—Life, pursue Happiness, Liberty—
Were given by God; they could foresee a need,
To limit man's power to rule over citizenry.

That a privilege to pursue does not mean
Outcomes the same; our right is the journey.
The documents protect citizens rights divinely;
Man cannot revoke these rights bestowed thee.

For if given from God, then not humanly;
If from God, then no man can revoke thee;
But if from government, then subserviently,
The people would no longer be free.

Through wisdom, experience, emboldened be
The patriots who fought revolutionary,
Spilling their blood to fight tyranny
And create a system not before seen.

A Republic to serve the citizenry,

With checks and balances to prevent tyranny,

To ensure government served, no monopoly

Be seized by a unanimous biased political party.

We understood that both freedom and liberty

Are indispensable for a people to be free,

And that certain world philosophies

Stranglehold these based on fear for security.

Through wisdom, our founders profoundly

Expressed the vision for people's equity

Based on the power of biblical morality,

Created a nation where all can escape poverty.

We taught our children, and so rightly,

That hard work, gratitude, and godly justice be

The requirements for all of our opportunities

To grow and reach our American dreams.

That to earn is better than to thieve,

For we respect it more than villainy,

Because, yes, we are an assimilated community

For godly morality and individual liberty.

Our defenders were revered, and we did agree

That assimilation was expected to bring unity;

Values were centered on Constitutional liberty.

We understood that true freedom is not free.

Then, as time passed, so did we.

And these heads spoke prevaricately:

That there are no winners, not even in victory.

That fairness and justice mean indistinguishably

Defining who it is we wish to be—

That if we think, act, or believe differently,

Then it only means that we lack equality—

And to be what it is we are to be

Means eliminating these discrepancies.

Tolerance is not to disagree and still love thee,

But to accept and participate without disparity,

Or else we fall into hate and bigotry.

That morality be damned for inclusivity

Of all desire and pleasure and depravity.

And a virtuous people really does mean

The abolition of God in all public things.

And that what we believe privately:

In order to save humanity

Be censored if it is found Godly,

In opposition to progressive, woke ideology.

These heads, which are floating free,

And the voice from the powers that be

Declare a world order of social democracy

And parrot "their truth" as if true truthfully,

That there is no absolute for life or morality;

That color is what defines so inherently;

And sensual pleasure promote ostentatiously;

And age restriction means intolerant bigotry;

And freedom to worship, freedom to speech,

And freedom to defend life and family,

And freedom to commerce, religious beliefs,

Is not liberty but bigotry and a lack of security.

And so many more they tell us to believe

And pretend that fiction is the Truth's story,

And by force and threat and bigotry,

They enforce this absolute so dogmatically.

That we are to celebrate how different we be,

That our melting pot is only about diversity,

That all cultures are what make us we,

And a single American culture is a travesty.

That one American language is inherently
Offensive, and it is a culture of supremacy.
For America to be great without bended knee
Is un-American, deplorable, and a fallacy.

That in order to be what we claim to be
As it comes to American Declaration speak—
A home of the brave and land of the free—
A place where all have the opportunity

To reach for our goals, accomplish our dreams,
Is only true if the ends justify the means.
That a privilege is a right entitled for free.
And Capital belief is only for Social belief elite.

Blind acceptance of all, chiefly those that see
A place to be welcomed and hopefully be
Alive in a land where they may become wealthy,
Yet still choose a path that is brazen and overtly

Adverse to how the rules are and should be.

Those who dun, conceal, waste resources we

Are told to lift up for party, gender, ethnicity;

For they are judged enlightened for profligacy.

These heads that we watch floating free

And those of whom progress adversely,

Forked tongue to conceal, edit, and delete,

We are told to believe without hesitancy.

They say choice means to be consequence-free,

And justice is biased about race, religion, belief

If those concepts could agendas defeat.

For modern righteousness demands self-pity.

And above the law, no one shall be

If they stand against their social ideology.

But those who belong are one in the party,

And the law is for peasants, not the elite.

For theory is championed, and it's been decreed
That color is worth and privilege and need,
And value is quality and color of breed—
To say content of character is inherent bigotry.

To have is admission and to be counted guilty,
But to take is to earn and promote solidarity.
To change is esteemed; to remain is unhealthy.
That morals be raped to evolve idly.

Commandments of gold, thou shalt not see
Because God-given is null if God there not be.
Separation a must, unless control be decreed.
Faithful, except the part where He made thee.

That prayer or belief, if the name Jesus it be,
"No other way to Heaven except through me."
Be unfair, offensive, exclusive, intolerantly
Declared by fundamentalist Jesus freaks.

Boasting of sin, our works, our "love" decrees.

Silenced, taboo, cross' religion culturally,

For death, pride, and fiction, we esteem;

Accountability, we hate as intolerant bigotry.

That phobic be applied to "anti" anything,

And action be affirmative if votes it can bring,

And values denied for signaling appease,

And "racist" be all of arguments steam.

That process is not due to you or to me,

If a claim is made by that of the queen.

Individual rights, terminate indiscriminately;

Their body, their choice—for me, not for thee.

Our feelings dictate science and morality.

For all foundations are truth: the new mentality.

To build is immoral; the world is our country,

And together we separate our individuality.

It is the highest guarantee that to truly be
One, we must celebrate our diversity.
By this, they do not mean our shared unity.
And then we shall find what it truly means

To be one of the brave and live with liberty,
Say the numerous heads floating free.
And to those who even slightly disagree,
That's where intolerant tolerance silences thee.

For misinformation disinformation be
Because obedience is virtue. And admittedly,
To question is dissent, and dissent is conspiracy.
Free press, free speech—free only as we decree.

To be an American in the land of the free
Means inadequacy and unqualified to lead.
To be the home of the brave means admittedly,
That at all times it is guilty of robbing liberty.

That to protect your own is an indignity.

And to put them first is indiscriminately

Abhorrent toward others deemed inadequately

Competent to survive without welfare policy.

That success and growth are numerically

Tied to the increase in poverty,

For then we will know government generosity

When fairness is skewed toward inequity.

This is now what we are told to believe

By the talking heads floating free,

As they redefine what it means to be

Tolerant, patriotic, and American religiosity.

Our values, identity, expired. Constitutionally

Outdated and flawed, they could not foresee

Technology, culture, how the future would be.

Morosophs correct Documents unsatisfactory.

But I refuse to degrade the brave and the free—
Those who bled and died for equal opportunity.
Ends will be different, like individual identity,
But you can chase your dream from sea to sea.

I refuse to ignore the truth of history.
Or, in emotional confusion, ruin my country.
I refuse to be ashamed of who God made me.
Or, bow before critical racist theory, ideology.

We have allowed what the founders foreseen,
As communist Khrushchev predicted slowly,
The socialist death of the American dream
And the eradication of God-given liberty.

I refuse to sit back, watch evil uproot blessings
That our nation's heroes have bled to give me:
A land of God-given Life, freedom, Liberty.
For in the dark the light will shine most brightly.

A melting pot assimilates to national identity.

Know each is free to practice what they believe,

Free from government, political, all tyranny.

And tolerance does not mean participating.

"They who can give up essential liberty

To obtain a little temporary safety,

Deserve neither liberty nor safety."

Americans understand freedom's not free.

There are activities that form American identity,

Such as free enterprise and personal liberty.

American's learn, not desecrate their history.

And a sign of gratitude most importantly:

An American does not, on bended knee,

Mock the sacrifice of his ancestry.

He salutes the stars and stripes—thirteen—

In honor of those who kept him free.

I pledge allegiance to the Flag of the United States of America, and to the Republic for which it stands, one Nation under God, indivisible, with Liberty and Justice for all.

"Religion, morality, and knowledge, being necessary to a good government and the happiness of mankind, schools and the means of education shall be forever encouraged."

The Northwest Ordinance, signed by many Founding Fathers, including George Washington

"The general principles on which the fathers achieved independence were the general principles of Christianity. I will avow that I then believed, and now believe, that those general principles of Christianity are as eternal and immutable as the existence and attributes of God."

John Adams

"In the chain of human events, the birthday of the nation is indissolubly linked with the birthday of the Savior. The Declaration of Independence laid the cornerstone of human government upon the first precepts of Christianity."

John Quincy Adams

"The moral principles and precepts found in the Scriptures ought to form the basis of all our civil constitutions and laws."

Noah Webster

"[T]he Christian religion… is the basis, or rather the source, of all genuine freedom in government… I am persuaded that no civil government of a republican form can exist and be durable in which the principles of Christianity have not a controlling influence."

Noah Webster

"[H]e is the best friend to American liberty who is the most sincere and active in promoting true and undefiled religion, and who sets himself with the greatest firmness to bear down profanity and immorality of every kind. Whoever is an avowed enemy of God, I scruple not to call him an enemy to his country."

John Witherspoon

"I . . . [rely] upon the merits of Jesus Christ for a pardon of all my sins."

Samuel Adams

"... the knowledge of the Gospel of Jesus Christ may be made known to all nations..."

Josiah Bartlett

"To the triune God – the Father, the Son, and the Holy Ghost – be ascribed all honor and dominion, forevermore – Amen."

Gunning Bedford

"Being a Christian… is a character which I prize far above all this world has or can boast."

Patrick Henry

"Let us enter on this important business under the idea that we are Christians on whom the eyes of the world are now turned... [L]et us earnestly call and beseech Him, for Christ's sake, to preside in our councils. . . . We can only depend on the all powerful influence of the Spirit of God, Whose Divine aid and assistance it becomes us as a Christian people most devoutly to implore."

Elias Boudinot

"... don't forget to be a Christian." (Letter to his son)

Jacob Broom

"Grateful to Almighty God for the blessings which, through Jesus Christ Our Lord, He had conferred on my beloved country in her emancipation..."

Charles Carroll

"Had the people, during the Revolution, had a suspicion of any attempt to war against Christianity, that Revolution would have been strangled in its cradle... In this age, there can be no substitute for Christianity... That was the religion of the founders of the republic and they expected it to remain the religion of their descendants."

Charles Carroll, Congress 1854

"[Governments] could not give the rights essential to happiness… We claim them from a higher source: from the King of kings, and Lord of all the earth."

John Dickinson

"As to Jesus of Nazareth, my opinion of whom you particularly desire, I think the system of morals and His religion as He left them to us, the best the world ever saw or is likely to see."

Benjamin Franklin

"…let us contemplate the blessings which have flowed from the unlimited grave and favor of offended Deity, that we are still permitted to enjoy the first of Heaven's blessings: the Gospel of Jesus Christ."

Elbridge Gerry

"I have sometimes thought there could not be a stronger testimony in favor of religion or against temporal enjoyments, even the most rational and manly, than for men who occupy the most honorable and gainful departments and [who] are rising in reputation and wealth, publicly to declare their unsatisfactoriness by becoming fervent advocates in the cause of Christ; and I wish you may give in your evidence in this way."

James Madison

"Sensible of the importance of Christian piety and virtue to the order and happiness of a state, I cannot but earnestly commend to you every measure for their support and encouragement."

John Hancock

"I am a real Christian – that is to say, a disciple of the doctrines of Jesus Christ."

Thomas Jefferson

"The great pillars of all government and of social life [are] virtue, morality, and religion. This is the armor, my friend, and this alone, that renders us invincible."

Patrick Henry

"It becomes a people publicly to acknowledge the over-ruling hand of Divine Providence and their dependence upon the Supreme Being as their Creator and Merciful Preserver . . . and with becoming humility and sincere repentance to supplicate the pardon that we may obtain forgiveness through the merits and mediation of our Lord and Savior Jesus Christ."

Samuel Huntington

"Providence has given to our people the choice of their rulers, and it is the duty as well as the privilege and interest of our Christian nation, to select and prefer Christians for their rulers."

John Jay

"The practice of morality being necessary for the well being of society... We all agree in the obligation of the moral principles of Jesus and nowhere will they be found delivered in greater purity than in His discourses."

Thomas Jefferson

"[I] . . . am endeavoring . . . to attend to my own duty only as a Christian. . . . let us take care that our Christianity, though put to the test . . . be not shaken, and that our love for things really good wax not cold."

William Samuel Johnson

"I give and bequeath my soul to Almighty God that gave it me, hoping that through the meritorious death and passion of our Savior and Redeemer Jesus Christ to receive absolution and remission for all my sins."

George Mason

"Bibles are strong protections. Where they abound, men cannot pursue wicked courses and at the same time enjoy quiet conscience."

James McHenry

"There must be religion. When that ligament is torn, society is disjointed and its members perish… [T] he most important of all lessons is the denunciation of ruin to every state that rejects the precepts of religion."

Gouverneur Morris

"With an awful reverence to the Great Almighty God, Creator of all mankind, being sick and weak in body but of sound mind and memory, thanks be given to Almighty God for the same."

John Morton

"We have no government armed with power capable of contending with human passions unbridled by morality and religion…Our Constitution was made only for a moral and religious people. It is wholly inadequate to the government of any other."

John Adams

"I believe the Bible to be the written word of God and to contain in it the whole rule of faith and manners."

Robert Treat Paine

"To the eternal and only true God be all honor and glory, now and forever. Amen!"

Charles Cotesworth Pinckney

"[T]he only means of establishing and perpetuating our republican forms of government is the universal education of our youth in the principles of Christianity by means of the Bible."

Benjamin Rush

"To the distinguished character of Patriot, it should be our highest glory to add the more distinguished character of Christian."

George Washington

"Here is my Creed. I believe in one God, the Creator of the Universe. That He governs it by His Providence. That He ought to be worshipped."

Benjamin Franklin

"I do not believe that the Constitution was the offspring of inspiration, but I am as satisfied that it is as much the work of a Divine Providence as any of the miracles recorded in the Old and New Testament."

Benjamin Rush

"The volume which he consulted more than any other was the Bible. It was his custom, at the commencement of every session of Congress, to purchase a copy of the Scriptures, to peruse it daily, and to present it to one of his children on his return"

(The Globe, Washington D.C., Aug. 15, 1837) speaking about Roger Sherman

"I believe that there is one only living and true God, existing in three persons, the Father, the Son, and the Holy Ghost, the same in substance, equal in power and glory."

Roger Sherman

"I am a Christian. I believe only in the Scriptures, and in Jesus Christ my Savior."

Charles Thomson

"Can the liberties of a nation be thought secure when we have removed their only firm basis, a conviction in the minds of the people that these liberties are the gift of God?"

Thomas Jefferson

"No people can be bound to acknowledge and adore the invisible Hand which conducts the affairs of men more than the people of the United States... We ought to be no less persuaded that the propitious [favorable] smiles of Heaven can never be expected on a nation which disregards the eternal rules of order and right which Heaven itself ordained."

George Washington

"Then I conclude, that believing a Providence we have the Foundation of all true Religion; for we should love and revere that Deity for his Goodness and thank him for his Benefits; we should adore him for his Wisdom, fear him for his Power, and pray to him for his Favour and Protection; and this Religion will be a Powerful Regulater of our Actions, give us Peace and Tranquility within our own Minds, and render us Benevolent, Useful and Beneficial to others."

Benjamin Franklin

"We have staked the whole of all our political institutions upon the capacity of mankind for self-government, upon the capacity of each and all of us to govern ourselves, to control ourselves, to sustain ourselves according to the Ten Commandments of God."

James Madison

"... [T]he Bible... should be read in our schools in preference to all other books..."

Benjamin Rush

"This great nation was founded by Christians... on the gospel of Jesus Christ."

Patrick Henry

"We hold these truths to be self-evident, that all men... are endowed by their Creator with certain unalienble Rights..."

Declaration of Independence

"The Bible is the rock on which this Republic stands."

Andrew Jackson

"The rights of man come not from the generosity of the state but from the hand of God."

John F. Kennedy

"In God we trust"

inscribed in the House and Senate

"Whenever a people or an institution forget its hard beginnings, it is beginning to decay."

Carl Sandburg

Quotes from:

*Archives.gov, Wallbuilders.com, Founders.archives.gov,
Allianceforreligiousfreedom.com, Revolutionary-war-and-beyond.com,
oll.libertyfund.org, USAheritage.org, aoc.gov,
AMERICA: if you can keep it (book by Josh C. Jones)*

SPECIAL NOTE

Please remember that if you like a book or an author's work, the best thing you can do to help the message, story, or author is to tell others. You can do this by leaving reviews and/or ratings on the online site where you purchased the material. By doing so, you help the book and/or author get more exposure and reach more people. This is something that not all authors will express publicly, but all authors do hope the reader will graciously do, and we are appreciative and grateful for it.

Thank you.